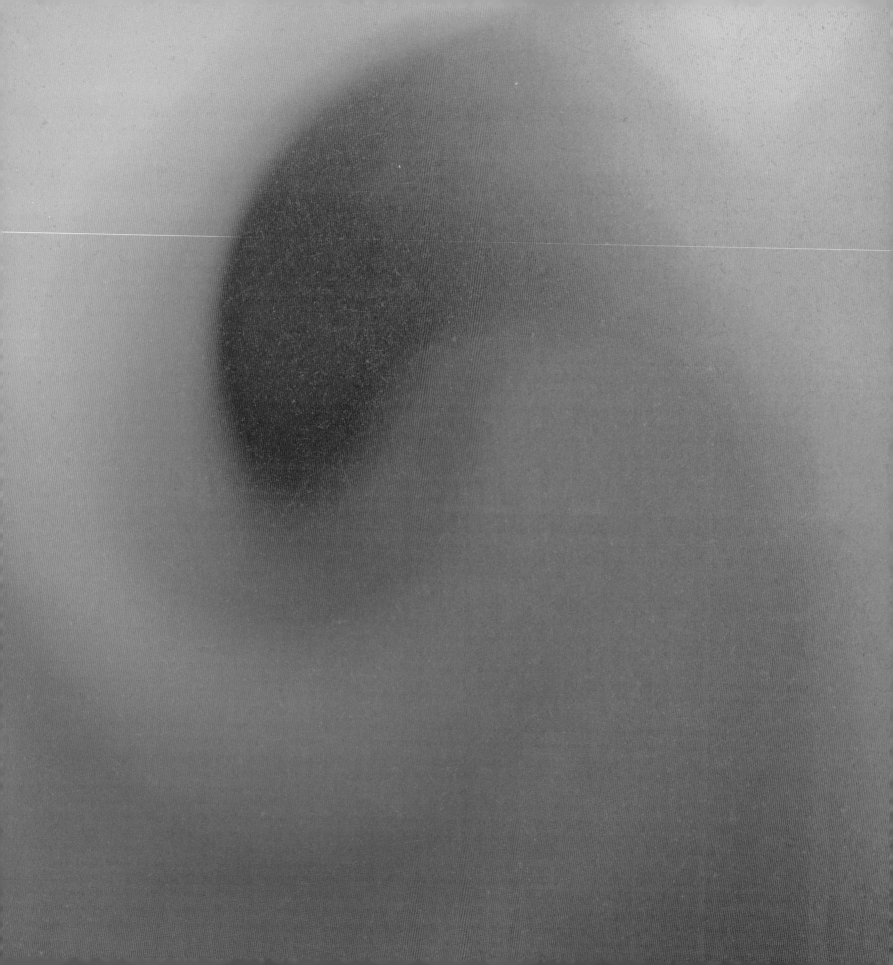

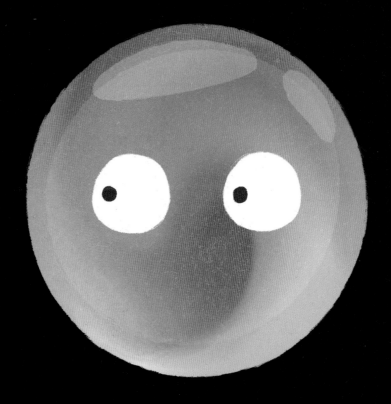

We Go Way Back

Idan Ben-Barak   Philip Bunting

ROARING BROOK PRESS

NEW YORK

Can ride a unicycle

Aspiring optometrist

Can move ears

Good at hide-and-seek

Tall

Likes cats

Hey, you! Yes, you!
We don't know much about you.
You might be tall or short,
have straight or curly hair.
You might like dancing,
or ponies, or cats.

Likes ponies

Likes dancing

Loves trees

Prasinophobic

Curly hair

Short

Can do a handstand

Straight hair

Does not like cats

A moose who can read

Forgot to wear clothes today

But we do know
that you are alive.

What is life?

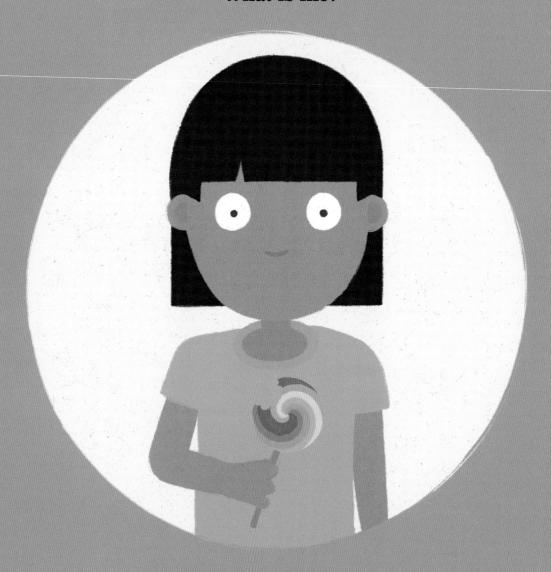

You have it.

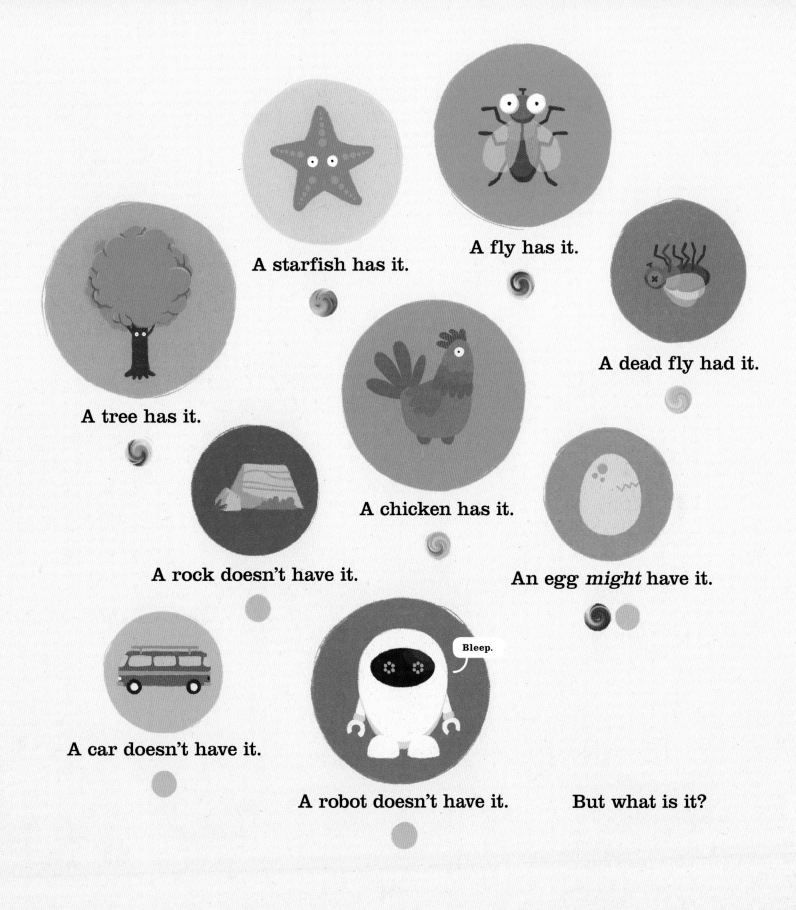

A starfish has it.

A fly has it.

A dead fly had it.

A tree has it.

A chicken has it.

A rock doesn't have it.

An egg *might* have it.

Bleep.

A car doesn't have it.

A robot doesn't have it.

But what is it?

"Animation!"

People have been trying
to say exactly what life is.
But it's not easy.

"Proteic structures."

"Magic!"

"Information."

"Expanding organization."

"A fluid."

"A kind of behavior."

"Energy."

"Self-reproduction
with variation!"

"A force."

"An autocatalytic
reactive set."

"A mechanism."

We know it's not a *thing*.

Life is . . .

Um . . .

Life Is the Way That Some Things Make More Things That Are a Lot Like Themselves but Sometimes a Little Bit Different.

Sort of.

Where did you get it?

You got it from your parents
when they made you.

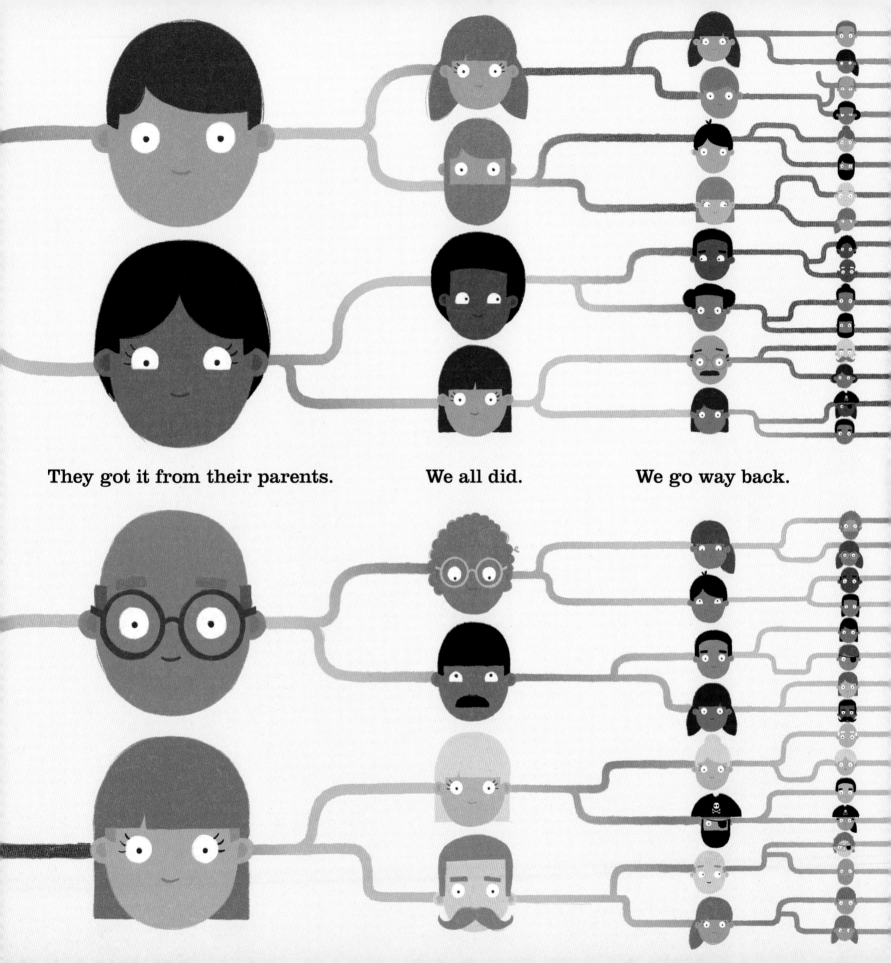

They got it from their parents.　　We all did.　　We go way back.

How did it start?

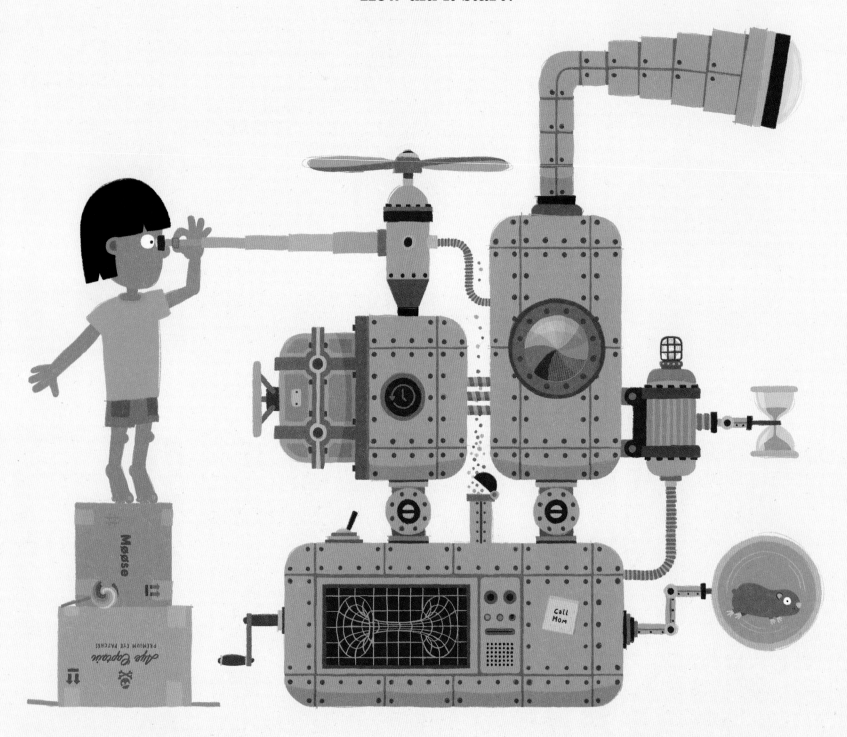

Suppose we could see back in time . . .

back to when the world looked like this.

It was just rocks and water then.
There were no people, or animals,
or trees, or plants.

But there was a lot going on.

Lava erupted from volcanoes.

Water flowed in seas and rivers.

Lightning and meteors rained down from above.

And then something odd happened.

We don't know exactly *where* it happened.

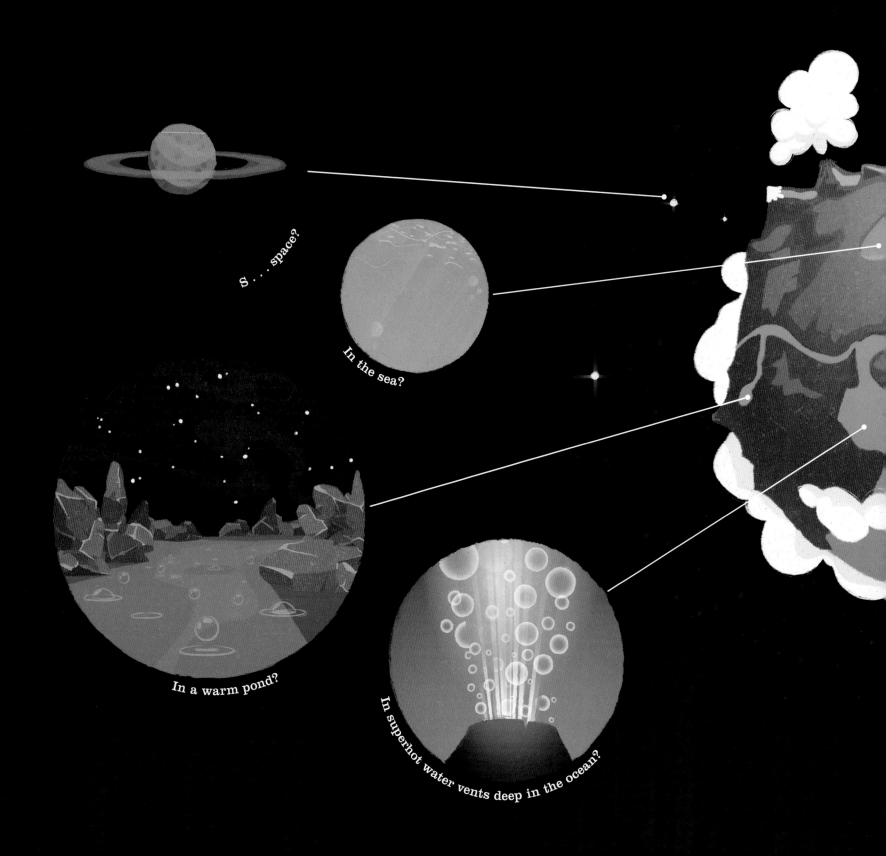

S . . . space?

In the sea?

In a warm pond?

In superhot water vents deep in the ocean?

We don't know exactly *how* it happened.

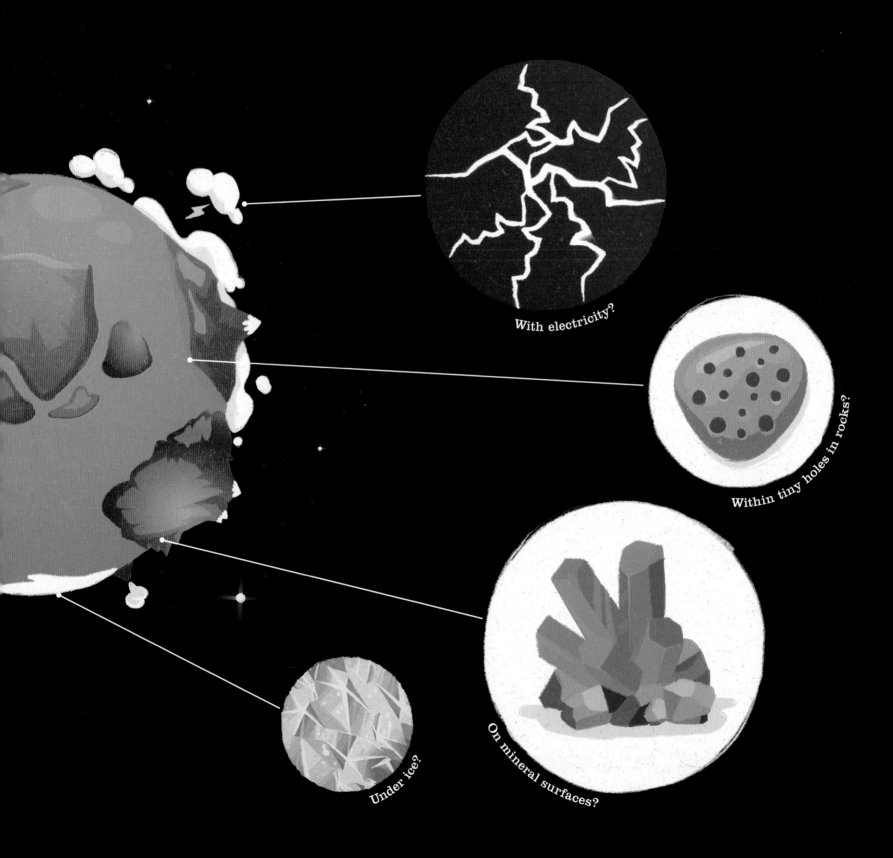

With electricity?

Within tiny holes in rocks?

On mineral surfaces?

Under ice?

But we do know there were elements
in the Earth's seas.

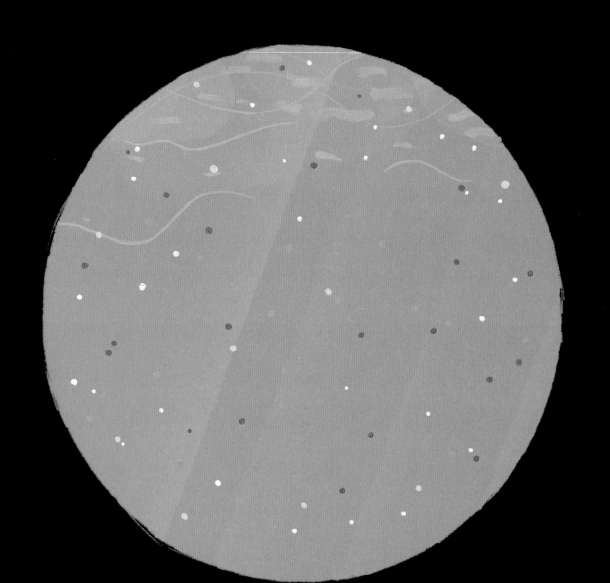

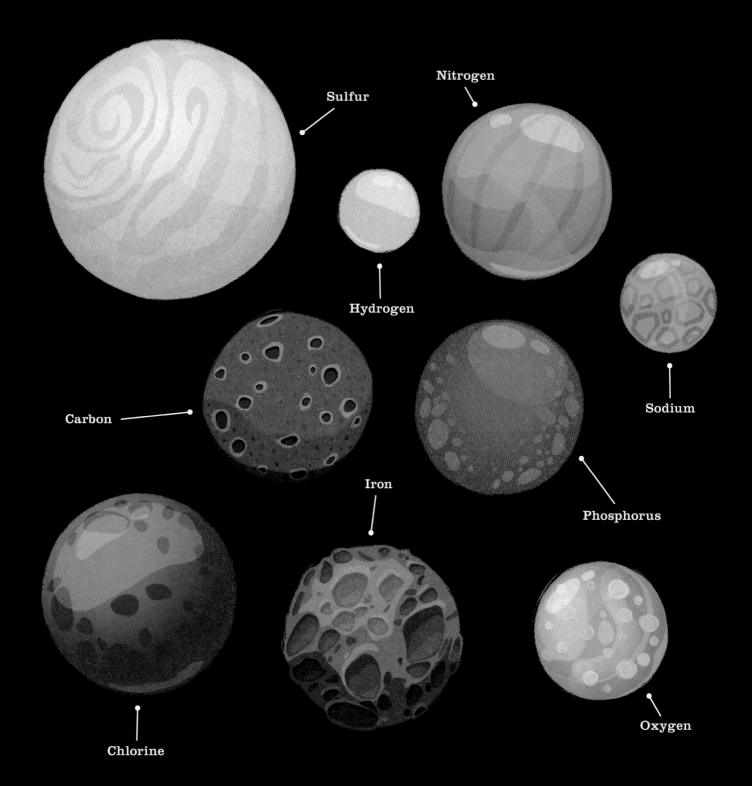

Some of these elements joined together
to form molecules.

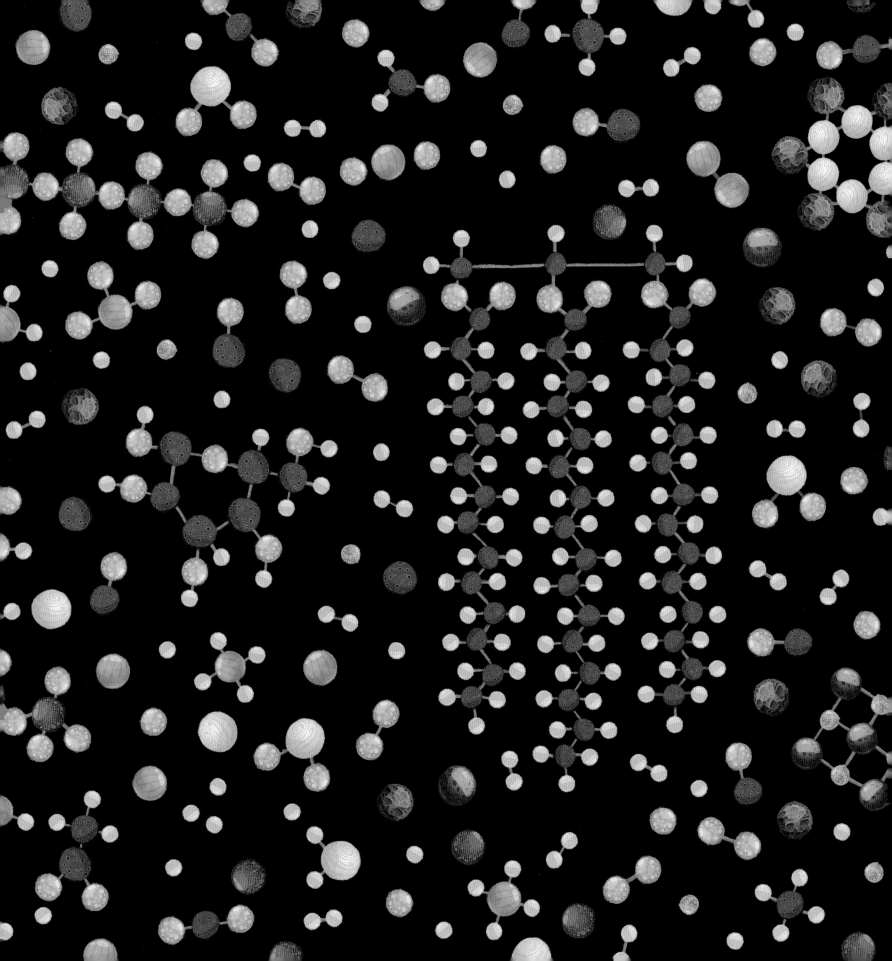

We know that some of these molecules flowed together to form small bubbles.

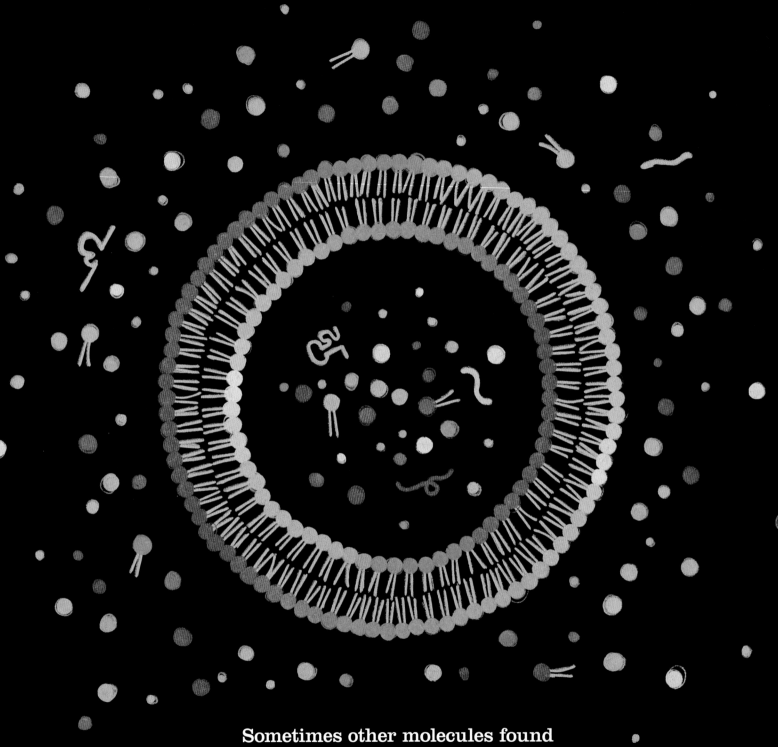

Sometimes other molecules found
themselves inside these bubbles.

And then one day, a special bubble formed.
This one was a very clever little bubble.

This Bubble Could Take Molecules Around It and Use Them to Make More Bubbles That Were a Lot Like Itself but Sometimes a Little Bit Different.

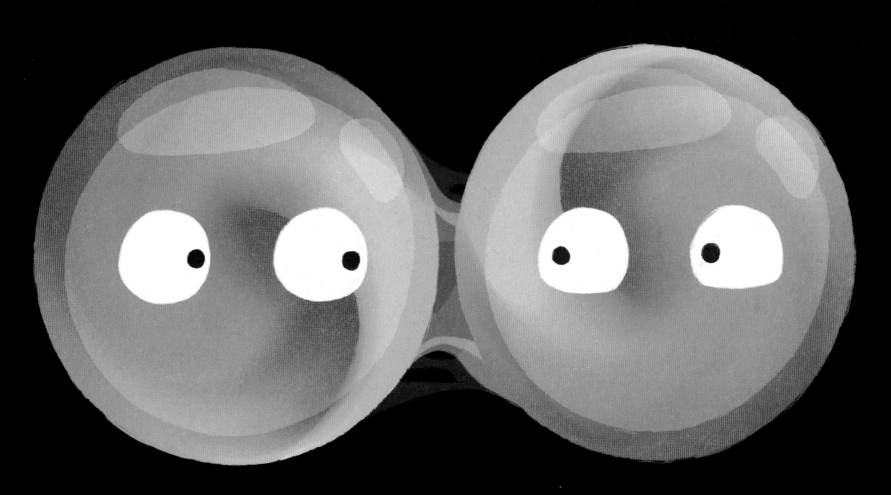

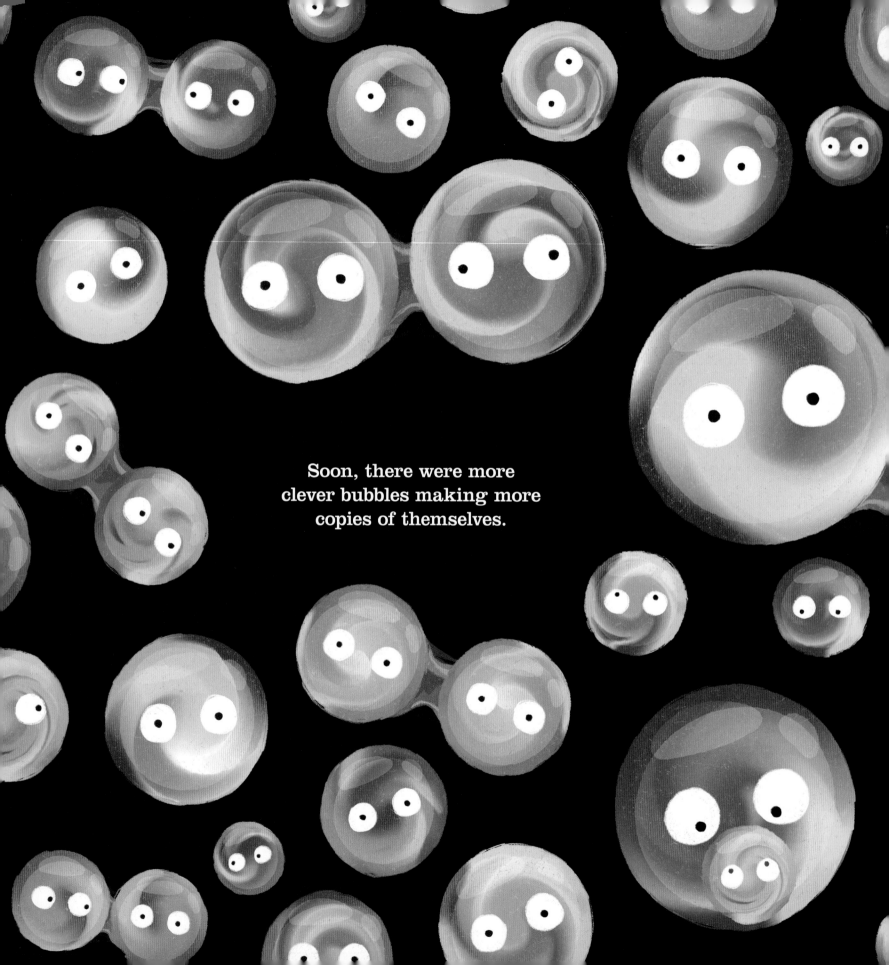

Soon, there were more
clever bubbles making more
copies of themselves.

And each was a Little Bit Different.

After a while* there were many kinds
of things wriggling around in the water.

*Literally billions of years

And each was a Little Bit Different.

In time, we found new shapes
to be in, new places we could go,
new ways to live.

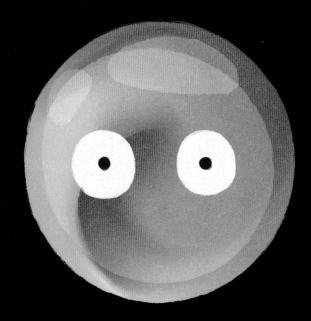

That first little bubble became

All of us.

Published by Roaring Brook Press
Roaring Brook Press is a division of Holtzbrinck Publishing Holdings Limited Partnership
120 Broadway, New York, NY 10271 • mackids.com

Our books may be purchased in bulk for promotional, educational, or business use. Please contact your local
bookseller or the Macmillan Corporate and Premium Sales Department at (800) 221-7945 ext. 5442 or by email at
MacmillanSpecialMarkets@macmillan.com.

Library of Congress Control Number: 2022910306

Originally published in Australia in 2021 by Allen & Unwin
First American edition, 2023

Printed in China by RR Donnelley Asia Printing Solutions Ltd., Dongguan City, Guangdong Province

ISBN 978-1-250-85079-9
1   3   5   7   9   10   8   6   4   2

All of us.